I0420895

Write 7,000 Words An Hour

Up Your Word Count & Get A Rough Draft In Under 10 Days

Contents

Contents

A Word From The Author

~~~~~~~~~~~~~~~~~~~~~~~~~~~~~~~

If you would like a FREE video version of this book, go here.
http://devlinblake.com/write_faster

~~~~~~~~~~~~~~~~~~~~~~~~~~~~~~~

Hi there,

Devlin Blake here.

What if I told you could write 7000 words an hour, even if you can't type at all? Sounds fantastic right?

I'll let you in on a secret. I can't type. I look down at the keyboard when I type. This is something you should never do. You probably already knew that. But I learned it the hard way, by really straining my neck. However, I didn't want to give up on my dream of writing. And I didn't have to.

It turns out knowing how to type doesn't matter.

You can't achieve 7000 words by typing.

Well, maybe you can if you're Barbara Blackburn, Guinness Book of World Records' typing champion. She can type 7500 an hour. But she was using a Dvorak Simplified Keyboard, and I bet you use a qwerty, like most writers.

A qwerty is your standard keyboard. I'm not even sure where you could find a Dvorak, although you could probably find one online if you tried.

For the rest of us who are not Barbara Blackburn, typing speed averages at 41 words per minute. That's about 2500 words an hour. Respectable, but not that great when you're trying to balance a writing job with your life.

So what's the secret to writing 7000 words and hour?

The first thing to do is to forget about typing completely and use talk to text software instead. Why is that better? The average person types about 41 words per minute, but speaks at a rate of 120 words per minute.

Good talk to text software can keep up with this, but your fingers probably can't.

Now you know the secret, but owning the software is only part of it. Just like buying running shoes is only a part of running a marathon.

So how fast can you expect to go with talk to text software? On a good day, I can write as many as 10,000 words in an hour. On a bad day, I can get out around 5000 words in an hour, which is still double the speed I can type at. *Well, double the speed an average person can type at anyway. We've already established I can't really type.*

Oh, in case you're wondering who I am and what makes me qualified: I am an author who writes under a variety of pen names. I have published two dozen books in various genres while maintaining a full time job. Horror is my newest genre. I have also decided to keep the name Devlin Blake for when I write about writing.

Specifically, I like writing about ways to make your writing faster and better so you can publish all the books you ever dream about.

This book was originally a part of a course I did on productivity titled 'Finding Time To Write'.

So, with that said, let's get started on getting you up to 7,000 words per hour.

Introduction

~~~~~~~~~~~~~~~~~~~~~~~~~~~~~~~~~~~~~~

I know. It's crazy to have an introduction when I've already had the word from the author. But that was to introduce me, and this is to introduce the concepts of the book.

There are some key things you have to understand. I'm not promising you can write your book in a day with this method even though it might sound that way.

After all, 7,000 + 8 hours=56,000 words.

Unfortunately, it doesn't quite work that way.

In order to write 7000 words an hour, you have to have a plan, and function at a very high level. It's impossible to function at an intensely high level for 8 hours a day, which is why I always recommend spending only an hour or two a day for writing. If you have more time to devote to your writing, make sure to work between appropriate breaks. This will keep your brain functioning at the required level.

I'm going to go over some mindset things in this book along with some light planning, as well as the best way to get results. Soon, you'll be writing at an elevated level and will be able to write your first draft. So, are you ready?

Your First Draft

~~~~~~~~~~~~~~~~~~~~~~~~~~~~~~~~~~

The first draft of anything is shit.— Ernest Hemingway

~~~~~~~~~~~~~~~~~~~~~~~~~~~~~~~~~~

When I talk about writing 7000 words an hour, I'm talking about writing the first draft, not a finished project. You want to write your first draft as quickly as possible, that's why talk to text software works so well. In this section, we'll take a look at first drafts, what they are, what they should be and why they are so important.

It's been said that the rougher the first draft, the better the final one. I'm not sure who said this, but based on some of my own experience and on what I have heard from other writers, it certainly sounds right. A rough draft will never be your masterpiece. Instead, it's the bones your masterpieces will hang from. (Hey, I'm a horror writer. You should have known I would have at least one phrase like that in this book.)

I like to think of the rough draft as a sketch. (I went to an art school). When you're sketching, you include all kinds of details that don't matter and skip over some details that do. You don't know which is which yet. That's why artists have a sketchpad filled with sketches of the exact same subject from different angles and with different details. When an artist goes to paint their masterpieces, they go back to the sketches and decide what to leave in and what to take out.

Without this preliminary work, the masterpiece would seem amateurish and poorly formed, just like a book.

Great artists paint masterpieces because they never censor their sketches. If they don't like something in the sketch, they pick up a different color using Conté Crayons or charcoal weight and just draw over it. You'll notice I talk about changing tools before they draw over it.

There's a reason they do it this way. They know that at a later date, they might decide they want that line back, so they change it in a way they can see both the old version and the new. It's rare for a good artist to use an eraser in the sketching phase..

One of the problems emerging authors tend to have is that they try to edit and write at the same time. That's actually the worst thing you can do for your book. Science has proven that the part of the brain that creates and the part that edits are completely different. They're not even located near each other. Nature did this on purpose because it knows you can't create and criticize at the same time.

That's why when you write a first draft, you should just keep writing as long as you can without stopping for any reason. You especially shouldn't stop to make corrections.

Now is not the time to figure out the perfect phrasing, detailed imagery, and brilliant metaphors.

You'll have time for that later, in subsequent drafts. Now is the time to sketch out your story. Figure out your characters, your plots and subplots, your big twist, your climax, the ending and where all the scenes go.

You don't even have to write scenes in a specific order. If there's a scene screaming at you to be written right now, but it's not what comes next in your story, write it anyway. Then write the title chapter- brief description of the scene. This lets you find it later and figure out where it really belongs.

And if you think of two different ways to say something, take a cue from the artist and write them both ways. Who knows, seeing them both together later might even give you the inspiration to find a third option.

This is your time to play, to have fun, to explore all the options for your story. When your rough draft is finished, you'll have something raw and pure. Only then can you refine it into something that makes sense.

Setting your mindset for this freedom is the first step in being able to write 7,000 words per hour.

Why Word Count Matters

You can't edit a blank page - Nora Roberts

You might be wondering, why bother writing fast if it's junk? The reason is simple. Whenever you write, it's not time or words you put down on the page that are valuable, even if they could win the Bulwer-Lytton Fiction Contest for the worst line ever.

Think of yourself as a great pianist, only with a keyboard instead of piano keys. All beginning pianists want to dress up in that fancy black outfit, sit in front of the grand piano and play for a packed house.

Writing words fast is like a pianist practicing scales. Each word trains your brain to write consistently, no matter what the conditions. Soon, this becomes a habit and once that happens, the words start flowing onto the page. Inspiration will come when you call for it. This way, when you're ready to play for that packed house, or rather, write your novel, you'll be able to do it with ease, fluidity, and enjoyment.

So how many words do you need to write in order to become great?

Well, writers' opinions vary on the exact amount, but most say at least a million.

Now, before you gasp, let me explain how a million words isn't really that much. It's not a million sentences or a million books, just a million words.

Consider this:

- If you write 5000 words a day, you'll reach a million in only 200 days.
- If you write 7000 words a day, you'll reach a million in only 142 days
- If you write 10,000 words a day, you'll reach a million in only 100 days

Think about that a moment. 100 days and you could be a great writer. That's faster than most schools and easier than most classes. After all, you're not writing some boring assignment or practicing monotonous scales. You're writing what you want to write about. You're just thinking of a better way to put it into words.

And I'll let you in on another secret.

You don't have to be a great writer to publish or to become a successful writer.

Twilight and Fifty Shades of Gray were not beautifully written books. I'm obviously not going into the merits of whether or not they were good books, because we all have an opinion on that. But the book's own fans agree that these are not greatly written books.

Here's a line from Twilight to prove it, just in case you've never read the books:

~~~~~~~~~~~~~~~~~~~~~~~~~~~~~~~~~~~~~~

"He leaned in slowly, the beeping noise accelerated wildly before his lips even touched me. But when they did, though with the most gentle of pressure, the beeping stopped altogether."

~~~~~~~~~~~~~~~~~~~~~~~~~~~~~~~~~~~~~~

You can most likely write as good as that. Especially if you practice writing 5,000-7,000 words every day. Practice makes great books.

And you don't have to be content just writing books. A book is 50,000 words, so it may seem pretty daunting when you're just starting out. But consider these other, shorter, story formats.

- Novels - 50,000 minimum word count
- Novella (a short novel) - between 10,000-49,000 words, but usually around 30,000.
- Short Story- 10,000 words or less. Most magazines prefer stories between 2,000-7,000
- Flash Fiction- 1,000 words or less.
- Twabbles- type of flash fiction told on Twitter. 140 characters or less.

If you practice writing this many words, then at the end of the year, you could have a couple of novels/novellas, dozens of short stories and hundreds of flash fictions. You could get published in magazines, on Kindle and print.

So isn't that worth a few scales, especially because you are doing what you love?

Plan And Get More Done

~~~~~~~~~~~~~~~~~~~~~~~~~~~~~~~~~~~~

True freedom is being easy in your harness –Robert Frost

~~~~~~~~~~~~~~~~~~~~~~~~~~~~~~~~~~~~

There are two types of writers: Planners and pansters. A planner is a person who outlines or plans their story in advance. A panster is a person who makes it up as they go along. This is known as writing by the seat of their pants.

I tried being a panster once. I wound up writing 5 first drafts of the same book. That's because the first few versions where boring and untrusting. And even though I wrote a million words (at least), I'm sure you wouldn't want to write a million boring and uninteresting ones.

Plus one of the secrets of being able to write 7,000 words per hour is to know in advance where your story will be going. Let's face it, right now you may have a few characters, a handful of scenes and some big gaps between them.

That's where planning comes in.

Now, there a lot of big names out there who say you don't need a structure or to have a plan. That's nonsense. All the greatest books in the world were planned. Victor Hugo wrote on Les Mis scenes on tiny slips of paper and shuffled them around until the story worked. The same was true for Tolstoy's novel War and Peace.

Great books take great planning. Even great renaissance painters sketched everything out in pencil before the brush ever touched the surface.

So why do we believe we don't need to have to plan? Mostly because we've been brainwashed into believing that that is not how an artist works. We have some mistaken idea that a muse should guide our words. We get this idea from TV and movies, and there are some big names there.

So why are they lying to us?

They aren't, at least they don't think they are. They claim they write without a plan and without a structure. But when you actually break down their writing processes, you notice that they have both in their stories.

Here's where the non-lie comes in. What these writers have actually accomplished is a way to internalize the entire process I'm explaining to you now. Because it's internalized, there's never an outside trace of it, so they can keep on believing their non-truths.

Think of it this way. There's a hundred pound box that needs to be picked up and moved. There are two people who can move it, a professional weightlifter and an ordinary person. The weightlifter will pick it up easily and say it wasn't that heavy. To him it's really not, because he lifts much more than that, much more often. However, just because he was able to pick it up effortlessly doesn't mean it wasn't heavy. It also doesn't mean that a person who has never lifted weights could lift it easily or at all.

It's impossible to internalize the process when you're just starting out. That's a skill that takes many books, just like lifting that heavy box easily required a lot of training beforehand.

Some authors, like James Patterson continue outlining to this day right out on paper. (and if you've never seen one of his outlines, let me tell you, they're works of art.)

An outline doesn't have to be one of those tedious ones they made us do in school. A creative outline only needs to be a sentence or two to show you where everything goes. I recommend a 4-part structure myself. The outline below is a simplified version I use for all my stories. It will work for any genre and for a story of any length. The use of the world 'I' signifies the characters.

- Intro (welcome to my world. It's got a problem.)
- Middle part I (I'm ignoring the problem, hoping it will go away. It doesn't, it gets worse.)
- Middle Part 2 (I try to take charge for the problem. But it's a MUCH bigger problem than I thought. I don't' think I can beat this.)
- Ending (I have overcome it (or not), the world is different now.)

Once you have your story loosely planned, the words will just flow from you lips onto that page. And since you know what's going to happen, this enables you to say it in the best way possible, allowing you to become the creative writer you wanted to be.

The Software

~~~~~~~~~~~~~~~~~~~~~~~~~~~~~~~~~~~~

Now let's talk about the software. There are two kinds of software you can use for voice recognition. There are others, but the two I'm going to talk about here are the two I'm most familiar with. Also these two integrate the most seamlessly with Microsoft Word. They are Dragon Dictate and Microsoft Talk To Text.

Before we go into the differences of each software, I want to discuss some generalities to help you get the most out of this software. We'll talk more about training for using the software in the next chapter.

So the big question is, how fast can you expect to go with a talk to text Software?

Like most answers in life, it depends.

As I said, on a good day, I can write as many as 10,000 words per hour. On a bad day, I can get out around 5000 words per hour, which is still double the speed that I can type at. This is why I've included three different sets or statistics in here. I'm talking about how fast you can write. I want to give an accurate overview of the high, medium, and low word counts. But even the low is pretty good. In order to type 5000 words per hour, you'll need to achieve typing speeds of 84 words a minute, which as we've already established is twice as fast as the average person types.

Take a look at the graphic below to see what writing at this speed looks like for your book.

- 5,000 + 1hr = a 50,000 word book in 10 days
- 7,000 + 1hr = a 50,000 word book in 7.5 days
- 10,000 + 1hr= a 50,000 word book in 5 days

Now that you truly see the potential, let's look at the two different softwares.

Dragon Dictate

Dragon is one of the oldest and most reliable talk to text softwares. It's the one I started with almost a decade ago. Back then, it was new and it didn't work as good as it does now. It had a lot of trouble understanding accents. Today, however, it figured out a way around that by using scripts.

Dragon comes with a lot of scripts, business letters, emails, parts of books and speeches. When you first get Dragon, you need to read some scripts to it. Don't go too fast and try to read it the way you'll dictate later. Since Dragon already knows what these words are, it's listens carefully to how you pronounce them. Once you finish reading the scripts, click the finish button and let it update its software. This can take a long time. Unless you have an entire day to work on it, you can't use the Dragon the same day you read to it.

Dragon's price is about $299. If you buy the physical version instead of the downloaded version, you'll get a Dragon approved wired headset. They also have other physical accessories such as a Dragon approved wireless Bluetooth microphone and a Dragon approved voice recorder.

The voice recorder is one of their newest and coolest features. You dictate into the recorder. Then, when you get home, you hook it up to your computer and Dragon will transcribe your words for you. Right now, it works about as good as the earlier Dragons. But it certainly works better than most I've seen.

Dragon also comes with the advanced options for customization. If you use a lot of unusual words, such as high fantasy, sci-fi, medical and jargon words, then you have the ability to type these words into the computer and read only those words to the Dragon. You do this so that when you say them in the dictation later it types the right word.

Microsoft Talk To Text

Now let's talk about Dragon's biggest rival, Microsoft talk to text. This came out around the time of windows 7. So if you have a Windows 7 or a newer computer, you probably already have it. *(I actually had mine for years before I realized it.)*

If you're wondering if your computer has it, go to start, search programs, and type in 'Speech Recognition'. This is what Microsoft calls it.

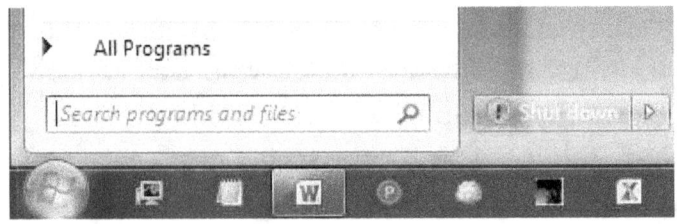

Then you should see a screen that looks like this. If you see it, congratulations, you have it.

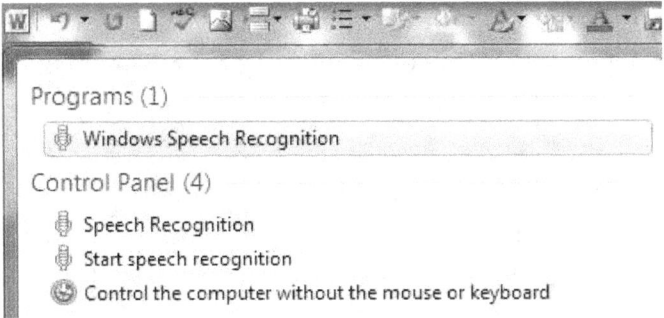

One of the best things about Microsoft talk to text is that it's ready to go right out of the box. The training you have to do for it is very minimal. You could train working with it and start writing with it at the same hours, which is one of the reasons it's my new favorite. (Sorry, Dragon.)

Of course, because you don't spend time training for it now, you will have to practice a little more as you go along. This is what I sometimes prefer as the accuracy is a little better. It lets you correct entire sentences at a time instead of only going word by word like Dragon does.

Microsoft also has a play-back feature, which lets you hear what you sound like to the software so you can train yourself to say certain words more clearly.

Microsoft talk to text is perfect if you have a more neutral accent or don't plan on using a voice recorder. (I've never tried it with a voice recorder, so I don't really know much about their compatibility.)

Microsoft version does have some customization options, but is not as versatile as Dragon is. Dragon lets you type in a strange word you want to use. However, Microsoft makes you spell it out loud using a phrase like 'A as apple' 'C as cat.' After you spell it out loud, it asks you how to pronounce it, and then it learns it. It's a much longer process.

So which one is actually best for you? The answer of course is that it depends on how you talk and how you plan to use it. If working with recording devices, strange words or if you have a heavy accent, Dragon might work better for you. If you only plan to diction on your computer, use normal sounding names and have a more neutral accent, then Microsoft's versions might work better for you. And if you have a newer model computer, you already have Microsoft's version.

Training for The Software

~~~~~~~~~~~~~~~~~~~~~~~~~~~~~~~~~~~~~

Now let's talk a little about how to train yourself for the software. Though the softwares do have their individual quirks, all talk to text software runs off the same fundamentally. It's these fundamentals that we'll look at in this chapter.

Have you ever heard a computer speak?

They sound slightly off, with no emotion or inflections in their tones. This is how a computer prefers you speak to it. You need to speak in an even tone, not too loud or too soft. You also want to keep your voice at an even pace, talking too fast or with inflections just confuses it. When the computer gets confused it either stops typing or starts typing nonsense words.

By far, the hardest thing to remember about talk to text software is to remember to speak the punctuation. You actually need to say the words: comma, period, new line, question mark, and new paragraph.

While this feels awkward in the beginning, it becomes second nature with time. In fact, it could become such a second nature that when you start doing webinars, you find yourself speaking the punctuation.

Avoid using it when you are suffering from allergies or a cold, or when your cat's in the room. The software learns form you each time you use it. If you train it with a nasally stuffed up voice that isn't' normal for you, then you'll have to untrain it later for your real voice.

This can take up way too much time and lead to unreadable first drafts.

Now let's talk about the best way to handle unusual names in your story. Talk to text software can recognize some names, but not all of them. This is especially true for people who have strange names.

The method I'm about to reveal is a method that has worked for me, but not one I've seen explained anywhere else.

I call it the blank method.

Choose a word not likely to show up in your story. I use the word 'blank', that's why I call this the blank method.

So whenever a character's name would be mentioned, I use the word 'bank'.

~~~~~~~~~~~~~~~~~~~~~~~~~~~~~~~~~~

EX: Blank picked up the urn and turned it over slowly

~~~~~~~~~~~~~~~~~~~~~~~~~~~~~~~~~~

Then, once the first draft is completely written with blank for the character's name, you go to control F. This is the find a certain feature in Microsoft word. Tell it to find 'Blank' then replace it with the right name.

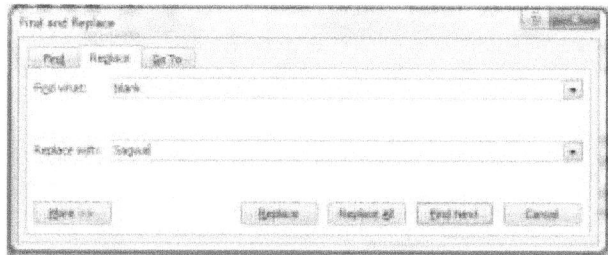

If you have more than one difficult name, you'll want to use a different word that won't show up in your story.

Or you could just use common names like Jane, or John. Every software will recognized these as names. Then you can just replace the names with the real names later.

Though they say practice makes perfect, no text to talk software will ever be perfect. But typing isn't either, so I'd rather be imperfect faster.

Your Isolator Space

~~~~~~~~~~~~~~~~~~~~~~~~~~~~~~~~

You've learned to use the software, you have your book somewhat planned out, so let's talk about HOW to achieve numbers like 7,000 words per hour.

It all starts with what I call your Isolator Space. I named it after the weird invention you see here.

It was invented in 1925 to usher in a new era of productivity and focus. It claimed to enable you to be 100% focused on the task at hand without being interrupted by any outside distractions.

Now that thing looks ridiculous, but it did have one thing right: in order to be   productive, you have to be in your own little cocoon world, not just ignore the distractions, but to be completely isolated from them.

That's why I call this mindset the Isolator space. Of course, this mindset can be difficult to achieve when you are actually distracted by everything. (After all, we don't have the advantage of the real Isolator and I don't think we'd want to wear one even if we did have it.)

But creating your own isolator space isn't that hard. First, you have to get rid of all the living distractions. The kids, the pets, the partner, no one should be in your isolator space. Shoo them away until you're done writing.

Next, you have to get rid of all tech-based distractions. Close the email, the Facebook, put the phone in another room or turn it off entirely.

TV and music should also be off. Not only is this noise distracting to you, it also distracts the software. The software can't understand you with background noise. Even though it's tempting to listen to music through headphones while writing, it's not recommended. Not only is it distracting, it also alters the pitch of your voice to match the song even when you aren't singing along. These pitch changes confuse the software and lead to the software writing a bunch of nonsense.

Now if you're the type who thinks distraction doesn't hurt, consider this.

'The zone' is a place where you're the most productive as a writer. It's also the most fun when you're in the zone. Once you're in there, any distractions can rip you right out of your zone, and it takes a long time to get back into it.

Researcher Gloria Mark of the University of California has found that it takes an average of 25 minutes to return to 'the zone' after an interruption. This goes for any interruption, even if it's the two-second interruption of your inbox dinging, and you choosing to ignore it.

Choosing to ignore something is still a decision that takes you out of your zone. That's why it's best to set up your own 'Isolator space' when you write.

Flexing The Muscles

~~~~~~~~~~~~~~~~~~~~~~~~~~~~~~~~

Writing fast, even with software, is like a muscle. You have to flex it in order for it to work well. When you first start, it's impossible to write for an entire hour using this method. This is something you need to build up to.

It starts with time boxing. This is where you set a timer and do nothing else until that time dings. Here are the steps to this.

Open a new word document. It's important that the document is clean so you can easily keep track of your word count. MS word does this easily. In most versions, it tells you your word count right at the bottom.

Set your timer for five minutes. It's tempting to want to do that whole hour now, but that's something that needs to be worked up to. Now, write for every second of those five minutes until the timer goes off. Then, lean back and see how much you've written. Don't feel bad if it isn't much right now or if many of the words are wrong. Both the accuracy and the word count are sure to improve over time.

A notebook is another good way to keep track of your word count. You'll want to keep track of the date, the amount of time and the words produced. Keep this up for at least a week.

At the end of the week, take out your notebook and compare the results from the beginning of the week with the end results to see how much faster you've gotten. In most cases, it will be significantly faster, sometimes even double or triple your previous time. Now that you're good at writing fast, it's time to add another five minutes and repeat the process. Then just rinse and repeat until you can write for a solid hour this way.

Final Thoughts

~~~~~~~~~~~~~~~~~~~~~~~~~~~~~~~~

So that's about it for now. If you follow the instructions in this book, you can finish your first draft faster than you ever thought was possible. This means you can write more in less time, and create any book you dream of.

Don't forget to leave a review if you liked this book.
http://devlinblake.com/review-7000-words-an-hour

Also, don't forget you can get the **free video version of this book** just by signing up on the website.
http://devlinblake.com/write_faster

And if you are looking for a website for both **inspiration and storycraft,** check out
http://devlinblake.com/

See you soon.

Copyright And Disclaimer

No part of this eBook may be reproduced or transmitted in any form or by any means, electronic or mechanical, including photocopying, recording or by any information storage and retrieval system, without written permission from the author.

The information provided is for general informational purposes only. While we try to keep the information up-to-date and correct, there are no representations or warranties, express or implied, about the completeness, accuracy, reliability, suitability or availability with respect to the information, products, services, or related graphics contained in this eBook for any purpose. Any use of this information is at your own risk.

The methods described within this eBook are based on the author's personal thoughts and experiences. They are not intended to be a definitive set of instructions for any project. You may discover there are other methods and materials to accomplish the same end result. Your results may vary depending on your accent, your motivation, your ability, and a whole plethora of other reasons. No results are guaranteed.

www.ingramcontent.com/pod-product-compliance
Lightning Source LLC
Chambersburg PA
CBHW072020290526
45787CB00013B/1537